Lilian Dring ARCA, FSDC

by courtesy of the Richmond Herald

Foreword
by Constance Howard

I can't remember when I first met Lilian but it must have been at a show by the Arts and Crafts Exhibition Society, the name of which was changed in 1961 to the Society of Designer/Craftsmen. I exhibited with the Society in 1945 so this was probably about the date of our meeting. Since then we have seen each other on many occasions. We visit in each other's homes and, having got to know her better over the years, I have come to respect her very lively, fertile mind. Her father's brother was an inventor and she has inherited his talents as she always has a profusion of ideas with which she cannot keep up. She has carried many of these out in fabrics and threads in designs that, in her earlier works, have been ahead of their time and consequently not always appreciated.

Lilian is not a person to ignore what she feels are attitudes or occurences about which protests should be made; showing her strong community spirit and awareness of environmental and social problems in some of her hangings, which are powerful in their imagery. She has been a fighter for things in which she believes and still fights on, but her attitude has mellowed with the years. Her exhibitions in public places and in her own home on waste, rubbish and war emphasise her great social conscience.

Trained as a graphic artist, Lilian's collages and embroideries are mainly pictorial, although some of her ecclesiastical work shows fine, abstract line design, with machine embroidery worked on her mother's old 1912 Frister-Rossman hand machine.

Some of her smaller, earlier embroideries have a great sense of humour, often with a subtle wit; her colour is usually low key and whatever she does has a reason, nothing is random. She may commemorate an event, may stress a social problem, may carry out a commission, thus giving purpose to everything that she does.

I had the pleasure of being one of the guests at Lilian's 80th birthday party this year. It was a very happy occasion, particularly for me, as she had displayed some of her work that I had not seen previously, and found most lively and original in comparison with other examples of embroidery of the early 30's that I remembered.

Lilian has an indomitable spirit that will not be quenched.

– Constance Howard
London, July 1988

Lilian with her older sisters Daisy (right) and Alice (left).

I am what I am

It was never Lilian Dring's intention to become an embroiderer. She has not in over fifty years ceased to think like the graphic designer she was trained to be and which circumstances beyond her control prevented. She has no formal instruction in needlework beyond what her mother taught her, belongs to no guilds or societies of embroiderers, and does not exhibit with them. She describes herself as a Designer/Embroiderer and is proud to be called a Designer/Craftsman. She is no respecter of rules and precepts and has never been in bondage to convention. She is an exceptionally fine draughtsman – a talent contemporary embroiderers may well envy. She does not start a piece of embroidery by making roughs and experimenting with colours, but goes straight to her materials, cutting, shaping and shifting them about in a predetermined area, until a perfect balance has been achieved. When it is finished she sometimes paints a picture of it for record purposes, for everything must be carefully documented and has its place.

Her's is not the embroidery of luxury but of frugality, and a discarded swatch of tailor's samples, a couple of worn out coats and an old felt hat are more to her taste than gold kid, metal threads and Thai silk (there is her famous Thrift Rug to prove it).

Her designs are essentially literary and should be "read" like the pages of a book, the lines of a poem or a stave of music. Her subjects and titles are carefully chosen. They relate to people and anniversaries (the Personal Pillows and Square Cushions); to her surroundings (Clapham Common from her studio window); to domestic architecture (the Fabric-House-Portraits); to contemporary political and social problems (Parables 1 and 2); to community and national projects (the Patchwork of the Century). Always ahead of the pack she exhibited a picture in imitation of stumpwork and a raised applique panel in London in 1935, and in 1950 entered an embroidered poster in an international competition, which prompts the thought that her embroideries are perhaps best described as Textile Graphics.

Old age is irksome. "I like youth better". The sideways glance: the rueful smile. Nevertheless, the poster for the exhibition she mounts each year for Midsummer Arts Day must be hung out in the porch again. "My house is small and there is much to see: please phone for an appointment." The friends and neighbours who came last year and the year before will be there again. When the last one has gone she will be exhausted, but to miss a year would be to break faith with herself, with her integrity as an artist, and this is unthinkable. Life has not been easy and recognition has come slowly. J.E.

A Rhyme of Time

When Lilian was born on 15 March 1908 her parents, George and Lily Welch, were living at Surbiton, Surrey, and in 1916 the family moved to New Malden.

At school she won all the drawing prizes and when she had her fourteenth birthday and a decision had to be made about her future education and training, they were strongly advised to send her to an art school. So an appointment was made for her father to take her to see the Principal of Kingston School of Art, Mr A J Collister. He looked at the work she had brought to show him and then said Yes, she could start at once – next Monday!

The subject on Monday morning was Plant Drawing. There were about ten other students sitting at individual desks in the big General Drawing room, the north wall of which was almost completely made of glass, and she was given a spray of sunflowers to draw. Recently she wrote: "In those days the formalities were strictly observed; we had something called Respect for our superiors, and the staff and students were not on Christian name terms." For a naturally shy girl it was a tremendous ordeal.

The master, Mr Clifford, a man of short stature with a very deep voice, usually prefaced his comments with "Not bad. Not bad at all, m'dear or me sonny" as the case demanded. His assistant, an ex-student called Miss Shearlock, had on a blue overall with hand embroidery here and there. She took the first year for Design, mainly basic border patterns and interlacing strapwork, as well as Still Life in watercolours. Other teachers included Graham Sutherland (not yet famous), Edward Dinkel, mural painter and glass engraver who also taught her at the Royal College of Art, and Lindsay Butterfield, one of Liberty's leading textile designers.

In 1923 a girl called Barbara Freeman, who was to become a life-long friend of Lilian's, arrived at the School. Together they were promoted to the Life Room (where Mr Collister inspected their sketchbooks every Thursday morning "hurling abuse and occasionally praise at all and sundry"), and admitted to the Special Drawing Group for students selected as potential material for the Board of Education Drawing examinations, the subjects for which were Antique, Anatomy, Life, Architecture, Perspective and Memory Drawing. It did little or nothing for their morale that the week of the examinations coincided with the General Strike, and it was only with the greatest difficulty that they arrived at Wimbledon School of Art on time each morning. Tired out at the end of the day they usually walked all the way home.

But her four years of hard work paid off. Thanks to an Exhibition gained through her good examination results, and with the help of a grant of £26 a year from Surrey County Council, she entered the Design School at the Royal College of Art on 14 October 1926.

She was one of the first four students to take Poster Design as her diploma subject and, having already experimented with lino-cutting, opted for Fabric Printing as her craft. When she graduated in 1929, Professor E W Tristram, Head of the Design School, foresaw a promising future before her, and she was offered a fourth year, but because of her mother's failing health, felt obliged to refuse it.

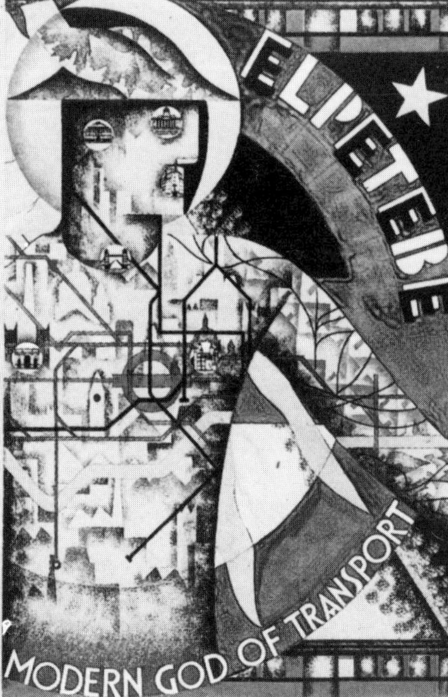

Even when she was still at the Royal College Lilian was fascinated by traffic, and in the early 1930's designed a poster that Frank Pick would have dearly liked to buy for the London Passenger Transport Board.

What Might Have Been

For Lilian the 1930's were "the lean, mean years", when all the talk was of depression, recession, dole queues and the gathering clouds of war. It was the worst possible time for a young free-lance graphic designer to establish herself. She had done some fine work at College and now, lugging her portfolio up and down Fleet Street, she showed her stuff to anybody who could be persuaded to look at it, but the answer was always the same: they liked her work but could not use it – at least not at present. Eventually she got a job in a press agency but hated it so much it was a relief to be asked to leave at the end of six months on the last-in-first-out principle.

In the midst of so many discouraging experiences it was good to see her poster for the Youth Hostels Association on a hoarding, and to know that had funds been available, Frank Pick would have bought the poster she offered him for the London Transport Passenger Board. For this she invented "Eltepebe", The Modern God of Transport, whose name she coined by adding four e's to the Board's initials. He stands in front of the Underground symbol, with his helmeted head silhouetted against her favourite sun/moon motif, and the serpent on the staff in his left hand ingeniously transformed into an Underground train. His features and body are marked with white circles enclosing minatures of well known London buildings, and along his arms which stretch out into the countryside, goes the travelling public between rows of red roofed houses. The original is now in the London Transport Museum where it was shown in 1985-86 in the Underground Women's Exhibition. It has been made into a postcard and in 1987 featured in the annual report of London Regional Transport.

Rag Dolls go Social Climbing

In 1931 Lilian married James Dring, a painter and potter. They lived at 32 South Side, Clapham Common, and when Christmas came round and there was no money to buy presents for their friends' children, she collected some scraps of material and old stockings, and made rag dolls for them. Everybody liked them and she began to cast around for a profitable way of using them. To the original dolls – Humpty Dumpty, Alice and a Guardsman ("Alice is marrying one of the Guards, / A Solider's life is terribly hard, says Alice") – she added a Cowboy, a Sailor and a Mermaid. When an architect who was designing modern houses in Gidea Park saw them, he asked her to make a set for the nursery in his Show House. It was fun, too, when staying with friends in Surrey and the expected guests did not arrive for dinner, to rush round the house gathering up bits here and there and make life size rag dolls to put on their empty chairs; and from this it was no trouble to make a life size model of Robert Donat in "The Ghost Goes West" with the idea of selling it to Gaumont British Films for publicity purposes. They were interested in the proposition, asked if she could do something similar but in low relief on a rigid background, and sent her away with a clip of Jessie Matthews in "Its Love Again" then nearing completion. Her presentation of the figure, the pose and the accurately placed padding, owe everything to her art school study of anatomy and life drawing. The beads and ornaments for the costume she found after long, trance-like sessions in contemplation of the jewellery counters in sundry Woolworth's shops. That she knew the figure was vulgar is indisputable, but it illustrates just how diligently she sought for ways of earning her living.

It comes as a relief to find there were better things in store for the Sailor and the Mermaid who became the subjects of her first raised applique picture. Unable as ever to resist a title with a hidden meaning, she called it "Deep Sea Fishing". Here, in her own words, is a description of how she made it:

I used a sand-coloured, white flecked remnant with a typical 1930's design for the background, and padded its lines and curves to become sea weed. I then built up the figures and fish into low relief with cotton wool. The clothes came next: dark blue velvet for the Sailor, pink and shot green velvet for the Mermaid; yellow chenille wool for her hair and bright orange for his hair and beard. The Mermaid's Purse suspended between them (the egg capsule of the dogfish) is covered in black leather cloth; the shells and limpets (you can see the barnacles on one of them) with speckled leather, and the fish (amongst the smallest two different types of shoaling fish can be detected) with various exotic fabrics. The bubbles are beads threaded on blue cotton. It is one of her most successful pieces and when exhibited found an immediate purchaser.

In 1947 she set about a process she describes as "raising the status" of the Rag Dolls in a picture entitled "Kindred Spirit". In the centre is a ring frame with a doll-like figure, one half of which is dressed in 17th century costume and the other in modern beach clothing. Similarly the arm attached to the hand that holds the frame on the left, has a full sleeve with slashing, ribbons and cuff of lace; while the one on the right is the plain, tight sleeve of utility clothes, a reminder that the war is only two years past and rationing still in force. The flowers on either side are in imitation of stumpwork; while the Kindred Spirit of the title is the 17th century poet, the Countess of Winchilsea, whose verse on the left of the scroll struck so strong a reaction Lilian's heart, that she wrote a reply to it on the opposite end. They read

My hand delights to trace unusual things,
And deviates from known and common ways.
Nor will in fading silks compose,
Faintly the inimitable rose,

and

O Kindred Spirit, I do agree.
Expression should be unhampered, free,
Admit few conceptions, keep less rules,
Be individual, not set in schools.

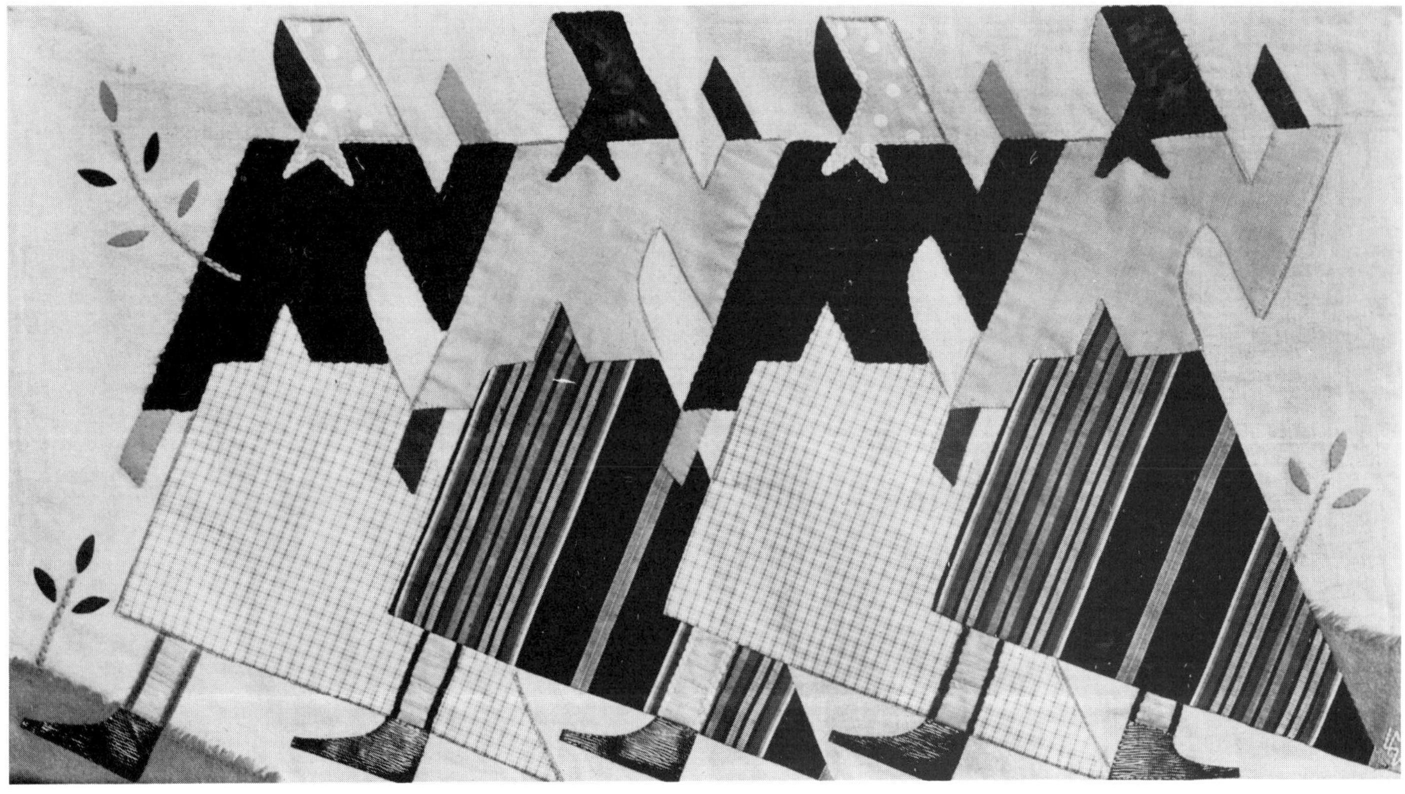

Peasant Dance

Peasant Dance

With some oddments left over from her Fabric Printing course, Lilian made curtains for the flat at Clapham Common, and a cover for an out-size cushion with a design she called "Peasant Dance". It was her first piece of hand stitched applique. Nevertheless, in the standard of the design, the contrasting textures of the materials, and the juxtapositioning of the colours it has a competent professionalism that is rarely if ever found amongst beginners.

The four figures have alternately striped and checked cotton skirts and jackets of black and orange felt arranged interchangeably with the skirts and kerchief. There are two shades of flesh colour for faces and hands, and for the boots she picked up some shreds of shiny black motor car hood material from her father's workshop floor.

She has no recollection of seeing work by students at the College who took embroidery as their craft subject, but now – judging by the nature of the design and the method of its execution – it seems likely that she took a look over her shoulder to see what was currently engaging the attention of the leading embroiderers. The result is immensely *decorative,* an adjective no perceptive "reader" of other Dring designs would think of first when trying to describe them, but at that time was very much used by the writers of books on modern embroidery; and indeed "Peasant Dance" is a once-off, the exception that proves the rule, an experiment that was not repeated. Henceforth she will go her own way, regardless of what embroiderers think or say about her (Rebecca Crompton was by no means the only one who was sharply critical of her work), happier by far amongst those with whom she had most in common, the members of the Arts and Crafts Exhibition Society, which she was invited to join in 1935, and to whose exhibitions (under its newer name the Society of Designer/Craftsmen) she is still an active contributor.

But the experiment paid off. She had found in applique the new artistic outlet for which she was searching, and the cushion cover became the precursor of her long line of Personal Pillows.

The design was admired by Mary Hogarth who, in and out of season, was constantly telling embroiderers their work should be "the invention of today in design and should express the present." One can only think that anyone who declared technique should be governed by design, would be likely to interest Lilian Dring. Be this as it may, Mary Hogarth advised her to send the design to J & P Coats in Glasgow who purchased it for display in Scottish schools. It then passed into the collection of the Needlework Development Scheme and is now in the possession of the Dundee School of Art.

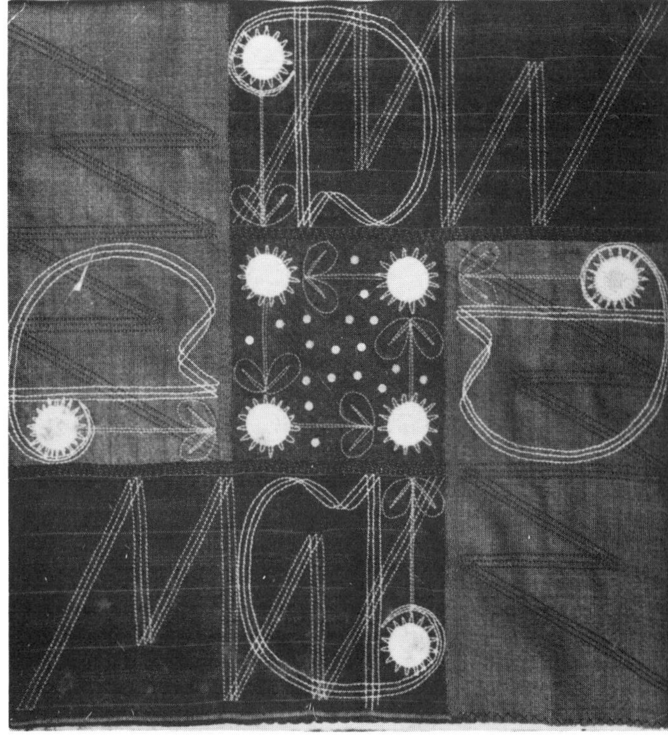

Personal Pillow for Daisy Welch

Margaret Johnston

Colour sketch from Margaret Johnston

Olive Napier & Olive Eaton

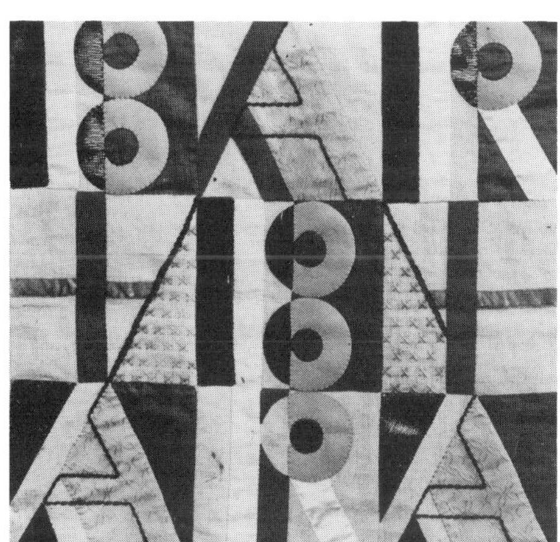

Barbara Freeman

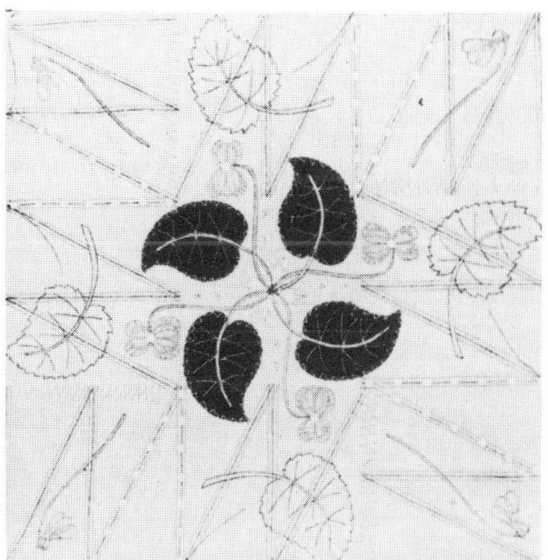

Violet Mills

Personal Pillows

Lilian once described her Personal Pillows as "an out-of-the-ordinary idea to replace the common cushion cover, in which the design is woven round the Christian Name or initials of the owner-to-be." And how typical of her literary style are those hyphens and the alliteration. She had played with letters and loved them since early childhood when she had a game called Word Making/Word Taking, and was one of those ever to be envied students who had Edward Johnston for lettering, calligraphy and heraldry at the Royal College. What more natural then that she should play games with her friends' names and initials?

She made the first one in 1932 for Barbara Freeman, and by 1936 there were others for Margaret Johnston nicknamed Johnny, Olive Napier, the same design serving for Olive Eaton also, and in 1947 there was one for Violet Mills. The designs were always made on a two way or a four way basis, that is to say, she either folded the background in half and worked the name in each half, one upside down or else folded it into four equal parts and put the name or initials in each part.

Whenever possible she introduced a symbol or emblem, and as an alternative to applique would sometimes use braids or cords, though for these a more graceful letter was required.

After the war when they became one of her best selling lines, she found it necessary to keep a record of the time she spent on a commission in order to calculate the price. Fortunately one of these has survived. It reads:

Design	Sun May 19	1.00 – 2.00	1	4 hours
		3.45 – 5.45	2	
		6.45 – 7.45	1	
Selecting Pieces	Wed May 22	2.45 – 4.45	2	7 hours
	Thurs May 23	12.00 – 1.30	1½	
		3.30 – 5.00	1½	
Arranging	Tues May 28	4.00 – 5.00	1	
		7.00 – 8.00	1	
Stitching	Wed	11.30 – 1.00	1½	10¾ hrs
		2.30 – 5.30	3	
	Thurs	12.30 – 1.30	1	
		2.30 – 3.45	1¼	
Finishing	Sun June 16	— —	1	
		4.30 – 5.30	1	
	Mon June 17	7.30 – 9.30	2	
Packing etc,		9.30 – 11.30	2	3 hours
	Tues	11.45 – 12.45	1	
		Approx total	*25 hours*	

Screen depicting Clapham Common.

Urban Landscape with Trees and Traffic

The last major embroidery Lilian tackled in what might be called her experimental period before the war, was a five fold screen with 18in wide panels on which she depicted the view from her top floor studio window over Clapham Common. She has it still as witness to how little the Common has changed in over fifty years.

The plots of grass were made from remnants picked up at John Lewis; the tree trunks from black rug wool untwisted into boughs, with the seasonal foliage behind ranging from light, spring-like green, through the colours of summer and autumn, to black lace at the top for winter bareness. The lace also came in handy for the wrought iron work on the bandstand.

The three ponds are represented in a ripple textured woollen fabric. The first (top left) reputedly the site of an old plague pit, with its central island where only the most stalwart trees are said to grow; the second (below the bandstand) on which model boats are sailed; and the third (top right) a paddling pool for small children.

Down at the bottom a row of white felt bollards and railings separates the road with its tramlines of round black elastic from the grass. The trams and buses are in shiny red frabric called Rexine, and the advertisements along the sides in a bubbly material to represent Lux flakes. This was her first picture with traffic and the church and brick house were her first buildings.

For anyone familiar with the Common everything is there, put down with poster-like simplicity and directness. It was finished in time to be shown at the Contemporary Georgians' exhibition, at the Wertheim Gallery, Burlington Gardens, in May 1937.

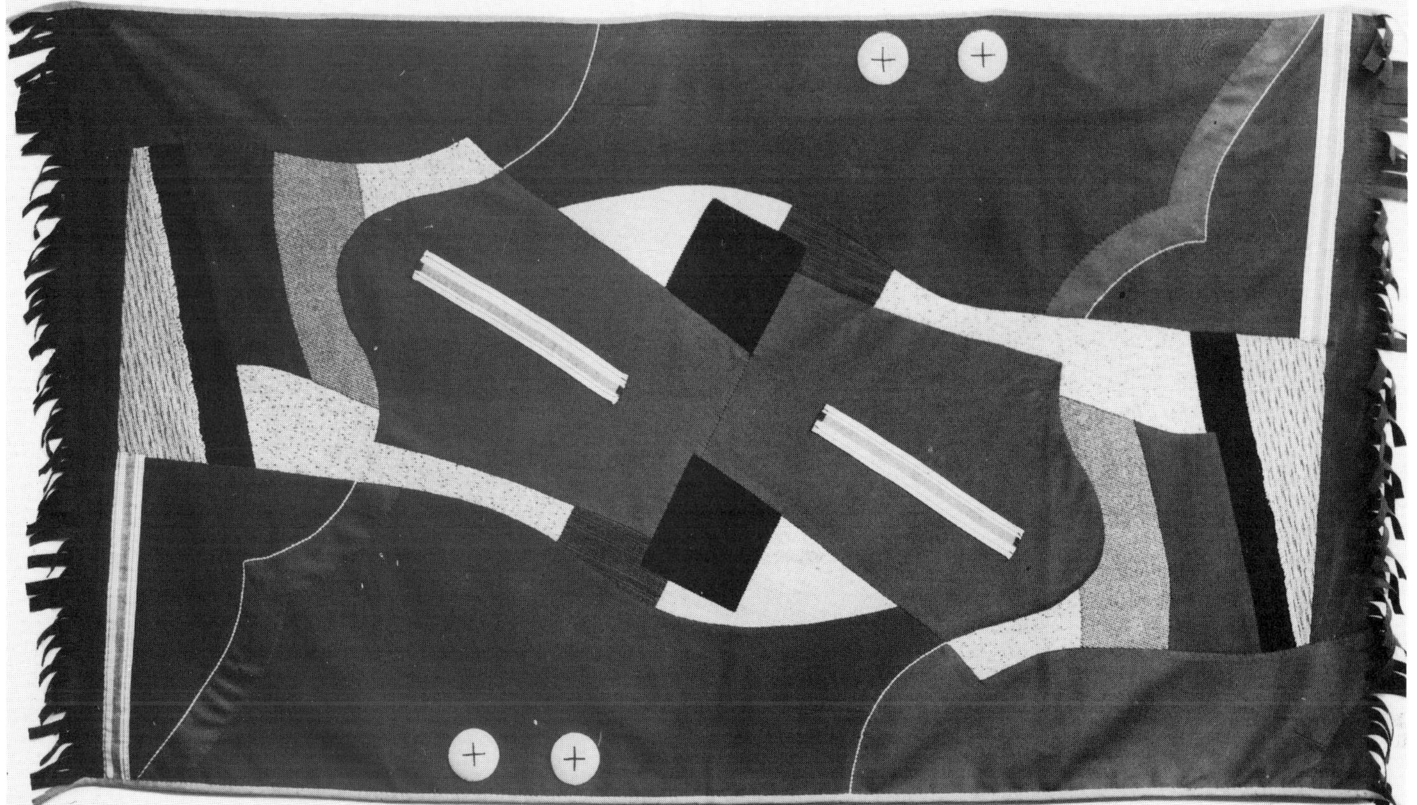
Thrift Rug

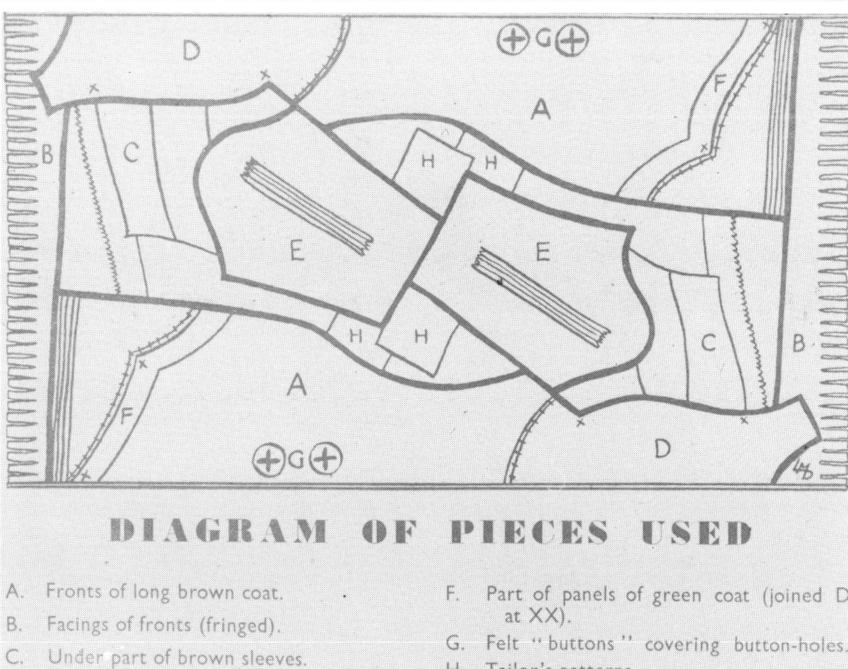

Line Drawing of Rug from Art and Craft Education.

Making Ends Meet

In 1934, needing a cover for a new divan, Lilian acquired an inexpensive length of woollen material, and decided to trim it with some shapes cut out of two old velour coats she happened to have by her. *"I was all set up to unpick the sleeves,"* she wrote recently, *"when I realised what a lot of material, time and effort would be saved if I simply cut away the material as close to the seams as I could get the scissors, and used the various parts – sleeves, fronts, backs and facings whole. So I did just that; laid out the released shapes on a 3 × 6ft space on the floor, and moved them about until I had a satisfactory design. I used the two fronts of both coats (one green and the other brown), the two green sleeves, and the brown front facings. One of them had buttonhole slits and these I used for the ends of the rug, cutting a fringed edge based upon the position of the buttonholes. I sewed the two buttonholes on the other front together, edge to edge, covering them with large circles of red felt, and repeating this on the other side, thus emphasising the reversing design that was emerging. The two green sleeves joined wrist to wrist, obligingly became a centrepiece, and I filled the remaining spaces with red felt, fawn and black scraps from the brown coat, and two narrow strips from the green one (it had shaped side panels), which I laid across the widest expanse of the brown fronts. The rest was simple. The shapes were stitched to the woollen background and the cover was in constant use at home and when we went camping until 1970. I called it my Thrift Rug.*

It has been reproduced several times the latest being by Constance Howard in *Twentieth Century Embroidery* Vol.1.

ART & CRAFT EDUCATION

OCTOBER 1939

INTRODUCING thriftcraft

TO-DAY, so many things are thrown away that could be successfully turned into something else. Our grandmothers knew the meaning of thrift—their discarded print dresses found their way into patchwork quilts, and their mantles, cloaks, and red flannel petticoats into rag rugs. Why not take a leaf out of grandma's album, and with a little more taste, and ingenuity, start making some useful and beautiful articles out of things that would otherwise be scrapped ?

How I began

Some years ago, I wanted several dolls for Christmas presents for small children. After some thought, I con-

Those whose fathers and uncles are tailors will be able to collect pattern bunches by the dozen, or a personal appeal to a local tailor would probably prevent him putting these valuable things into the dustbin. Lastly, collect a few milk bottle caps. Washed, with the rim cut off, and the impressed lettering rubbed down with a knife handle, these flat silver discs can be cut into shapes—stars, flowers, etc.

The General Idea

Imagination goes a long way in this craft, especially when it comes to the pictorial side. Begin to *look* at materials and see what they *suggest* to you. You will

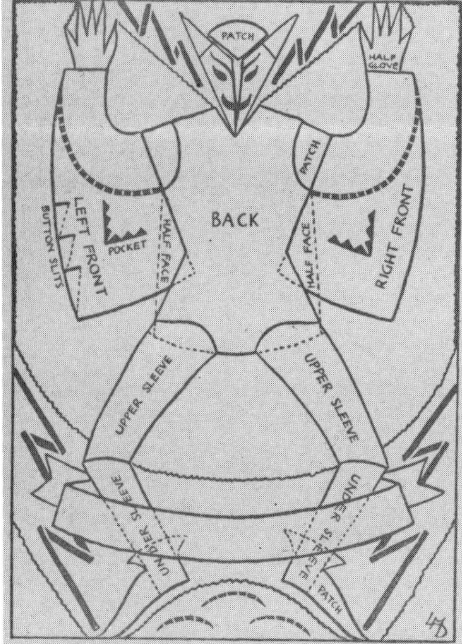

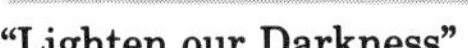
"Lighten our Darkness"

"Darken our Lightness"

Embroidered Geography

"Thriftcraft"

During September and October 1939 the *Teachers' World and Schoolmistress* printed three articles by Lilian entitled "Ideas for Craft Lessons"; and between September 1939 and June 1940 *Art and Craft Education* (whose circulation extended to Australia and New Zealand), carried a series of eight articles for which she coined the title "Thriftcraft". With the outbreak of the war her squirrel collection of scraps and remnants, the Rag Dolls, Thrift Rug and Personal Pillows had come into their own, and it was gratifying to find that editors were now only too happy to number her amongst their contributors. Unfortunately the paper on which the diagrams and illustrations she drew to accompany the articles were printed was of poor quality and those reproduced here are unavoidably faint.

Her object in preparing the articles was primarily to impress upon art, craft and needlework teachers the importance of finding ingenious ways of using waste materials, for, with so many things threatened with destruction and an already apparent lack of supplies, she reckoned it was all the more important for the creative instinct in children to be fostered and encouraged.

Of "Thriftcraft" she writes: *Imagination goes a long way in this craft. Begin to* **look** *at materials and see what they suggest to you. You will find endless possibilities. Tweeds looking like brickwork, fields, mountains. Search for silks and cottons that suggest animals, fish, water, skies. Old clothes must, of course, be used with discretion. Very worn parts cut away, or tactfully covered with other materials. Please,* **never** *sew on a button just as a piece of decoration, or "because it wants something there". Always have a reason for everything. Stitches should be kept as simple as possible. I use few but the ordinary sewing stitches – hemming, over-sewing, herring-boning, etc. Couching is useful and very easy.*

There are clear instructions and diagrams for the Rag Dolls and the Thrift Rug, but the Personal Pillows have been simplified and are now "Cushions of the Country". She writes: *"The simple square shape is, I think, one of the most successful, and I give four suggestions for square-filling that can be carried out in the simplest applique and stitchery. The applied shapes are easy to cut out, and in each case repeat on either side of a central stem"*. What she omits to say is that the thistle started life on Margaret Johnston's Personal Pillow.

She is very preoccupied with the depressing effect of blackout curtains and suggests ways of brightening them up. There is, for example, an angel with a scroll saying "Lighten Our Darkness" paired with a demon who has one with "Darken our Lightness". The messages are to be written out first on paper, traced onto the scroll, and then outlined with a continuous length of wool or string.

Like all good calligraphers she is fascinated by the continuous line, and in one of the articles she gives interesting directions for outlining the figure of Thisbe as

Cushions of the Country

she tries to kiss Pyramus through the hole in a tweedy brick wall. It is first to be marked onto the background in chalk and the wool pinned to this at intervals. *If the illustration is studied carefully,* she writes, *it will be seen that one end of the outline starts with her back curl, outlines her head and face, continuing down her left and up her right side, ending eventually in her side curls, and is finally divided to suggest the eye.* We are to take a pencil and endeavour to follow the various lines from beginning to end.

In 1945 she used the same calligraphic device for the figure on a panel called "Peace . . ." with an exploding atom bomb on either side and the world in flames below.

Finally she draws attention to the possibility of combining ordinary lessons – in this instance physical geography – with needlework. First, there is the background to be made. The scraps are to be separated into colours, and then sub-divided into lights and darks of each colour. These are then to be joined into strips and sewn together one below the other in this order: pale blues, for sky; pale greys and fawns – clouds; pinks and yellows – sunlights; purples – mountains; dark greens – hills; dark blues – rivers; pale greens – grass; brown – ploughed fields; reds – subsoil; black – strata. On top of them goes a tree of rug wool with a leafy outline in pale green, a few large faggoting stitches between the branches, and some diagonal rows of button-holing to suggest ploughed earth.

What these articles reveal, most clearly is that Lilian would have made a good teacher of children of all ages; and what sympathy she has with teachers deprived of their normal materials. *I am only too well aware,* she wrote, *that overwork and overcrowding are not conducive to good ideas, but they can thrive on lack of materials and reveal unknown sources of inventiveness, thus bringing out the personality of the individual.* She still holds to this opinion.

● "Peace and . . ."

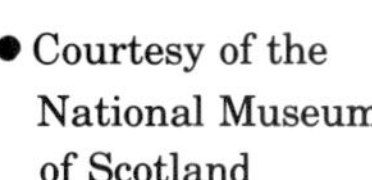
● Courtesy of the National Museum of Scotland

● Pyramus and Thisbe

Parable I Courtesy of the National Museum of Scotland

Parable 1 1941

In 1941 Lilian, hurling her materials together with an urgency provoked by her subject, made a statement about World War II that has no parallel in the annals of 20th century embroidery. She described it as a Parable.

Tonight, in The Heavens Above, the German bombers have crossed the Channel and the RAF has gone up to beat them off. There are dog fights, bursting shells and barrage ballons. In the Earth Beneath, a great darkness, a rolling pall of bitter, black smoke, bombed out roofless houses and churches without so much as a splinter of glass in the windows. The ambulances have arrived, people will be dug out of the ruins, fire engines with long ladders and men with hatchets and hoses will be here soon. There is sure to be a First Aid post round the corner and the WVS pouring out cups of tea. Part time ARP Warden, Mrs Lilian Dring, put it all down exactly as she saw it in applique embroidery.

In the Shelters Under the Earth neighbours are sleeping in layers, just like Henry Moore drew them. They came down the escalators last evening clutching gas masks, a few creature comforts and a child's toy. They will go back up them again at first light. To what? Nobody knows. A home in ruins? or a sigh of relief? That they will be back tomorrow night, is certain.

Lilian made this hanging for a bombed out window, and showed it with the Arts and Craft Exhibition Society in 1941. It was purchased in 1945 for the Needlework Development Scheme and is now in the Royal Scottish Museum, Edinburgh.

An official catalogue entry describes it in terms of threads, stitches and colours and reads:

Black, white, purple, fawn, yellow, brown, pale brown, pale green, blue-green, grey, pinkish-brown, blue, dark blue, pale blue, red-brown, and purple-red woollen threads; white cotton thread; grey and black silk(?) braid; white cotton cord; bugles, sequins, buttons and applied leather; net, linen and black- glazed cloth; on a ground of square and rectangular pieces of different woollen materials joined to a white cotton lining with black and white threads. Mainly couched work with blanket, fly and running stitches; the materials of the ground joined with herringbone stitch. The panel is backed with linen and edged with black linen tape. Along the top are bone rings for hanging.

Visitors to the Festival of Britain admiring the Patchwork of the Century

Patchwork of the Century

At 3 pm on 25 June 1951 Dame Sybil Thorndike opened an exhibition at York House, Twickenham entitled Women of the Century 1851-1951. Its object was to illustrate the history of the social and political advancement achieved by women during the past century by means of pictures, photographs, models, costume, furnishings, embroidery, etc. Lilian was the Display Organiser.

Careful at all times to keep material related in any way to her work, Lilian still has the mock-up she made for the catalogue, including her pencil sketch for the cover, the first block pull of the figure, the finished print, and a sample of the paper. Here are the names of the 26 members of the Executive Committee, and a list of the participating women's organisations. It is one of the those invaluable little gems for which local historians are constantly searching. The Introduction ends with some

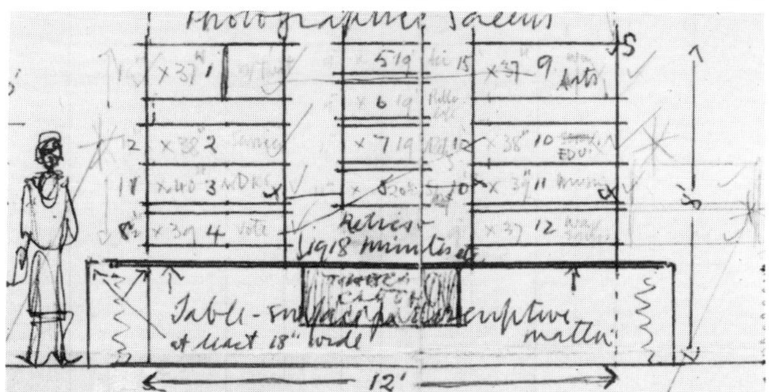

words by Olive Schreiner, the poet of the women's movement:

And he said, Have you seen the locusts
how they cross a stream?
First one comes down to the water-edge,
and it is swept away, and then another comes,
and at last with their bodies piled up
a bridge is built, and the rest pass over.
And she said, Over that bridge which is built
with our bodies, who shall pass?
And he said, The entire human race.
And the woman grasped her staff.
And I saw her turn down that dark path
to the river.

Never one to miss the opportunity to foster good community relationships, Lilian also organised the making of a huge hanging for the exhibition which she called Patchwork of the Century. It is 10 ft square and consists of 100 squares embroidered by 80 members of various local women's organisations. Each has a motif related to some important event or person associated with a particular decade. Lilian herself worked four of them including the first, a picture of the Crystal Palace, and the last, entitled Building the South Bank. She was, of course, responsible for most of the designs, though a few women made their own. She still has the chart she made showing the embroiderer's name, organisation, and subject of the design. There is a note on it in her writing which says "Worked in separate squares in 2 months – April – June 1951."

When the exhibition closed the hanging was transferred to the Festival of Britain Exhibition and placed in the Tank Room at the based of the Shot Tower through which visitors passed after viewing the 1851 Pavilion. It attracted a good deal of favourable comment from the press.

In October 1968 it was displayed by Lilian in her home

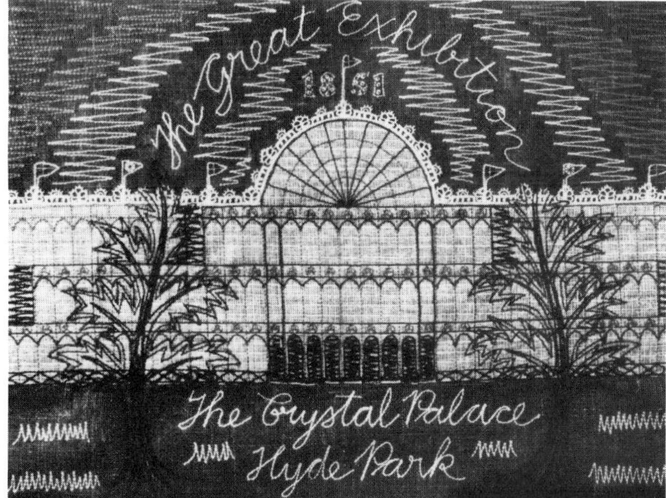

at Hampton Road, Teddington, for the Golden Jubilee celebrations of the Teddington and Hampton Women Citizens' Association. On this occasion she made a careful plan for showing it on graph paper of which the central section is illustrated here and in 1976 it was included in the exhibition – Tonic for the Nation – at the Victoria and Albert Museum. In 1984 she presented it to the Festival Hall where it hangs on the sixth floor.

European Recovery Programme Poster

Cushions for Coronation of (a) Edward VIII and (b) George VI

a

b

Anglo-American Cushion

Colour sketch from American Cushion

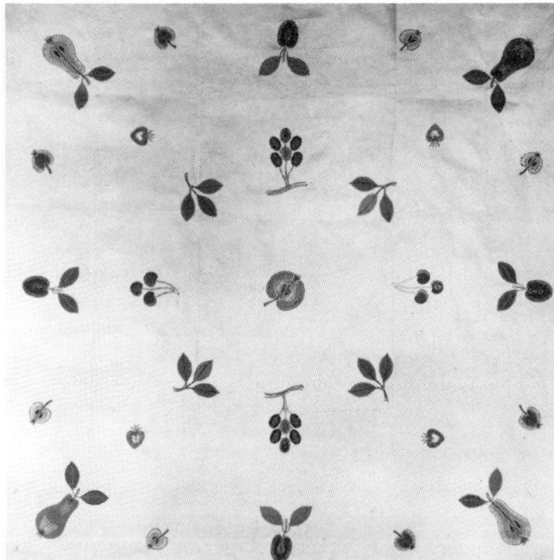

Detail of Design on a Bedspread

National International Affairs

Throughout her life Lilian has lived fully in her generation and, like a good poster artist, has kept a sharp eye on the passing show. In 1936, therefore, when all the talk was of the coronation of Edward VIII, she made her first Square Cushion in anticipation of it, quickly withdrawing it and replacing it with one for George VI when the Abdication occurred. Although of comparatively small aesthetic interest they led to her finding a new subject in the European Recovery Programme, better remembered today as Marshall Aid, and the making of a third Square Cushion for a British Council Travelling Exhibition aimed at promoting good relationships between Britain, the United States and Canada. She still has the watercolour sketch she made after finishing it. In addition she made bedspreads at the request of John Farleigh for the British Handcrafts Export Scheme.

Still in this vein, she made a needlework poster in which the initials ERP form the central motif, with threads passing through the R to indicate the countries benefitting from Marshall Aid. She submitted it to the British Section of an international competition and was awarded a prize, but a technicality over which members of the jury failed to agree, prevented them from giving it more than fourth place. In it she successfully merged her poster art with her understanding of machine stitched applique, and it seems to me that her position is now analagous to that of a person who, having studied a language and learnt to speak it with a degree of confidence, suddenly finds they can also think in it.

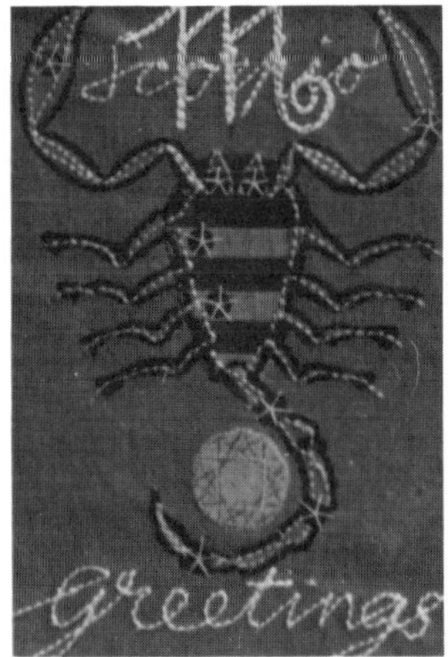

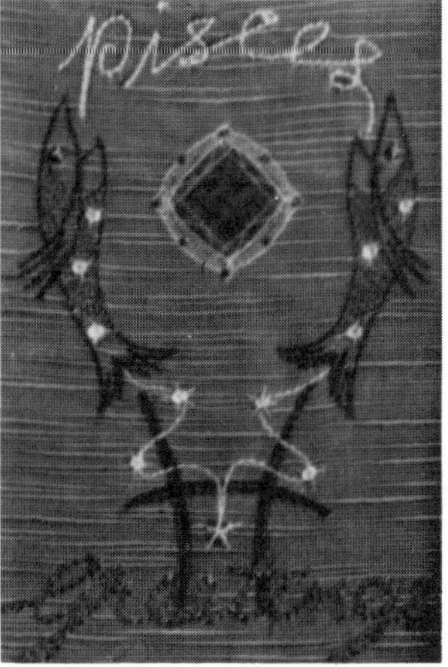

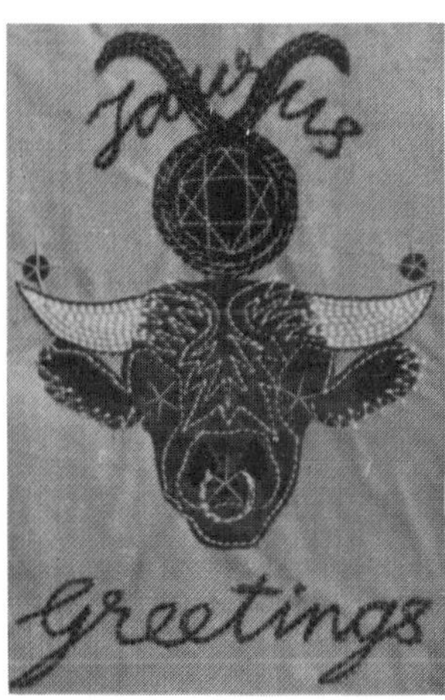

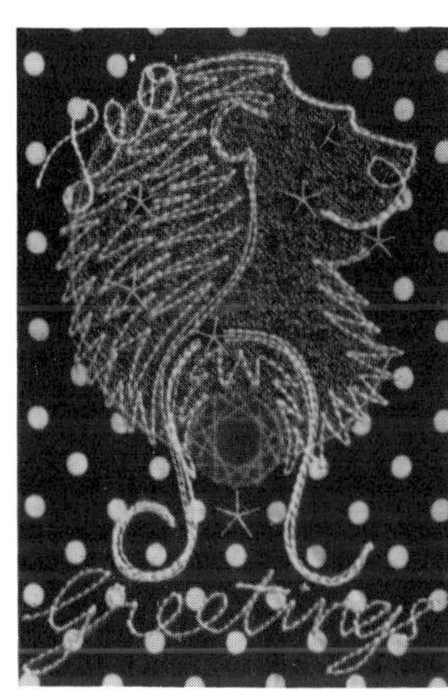

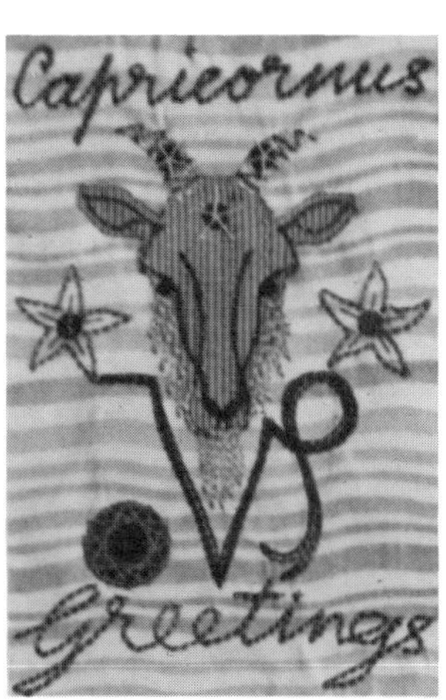

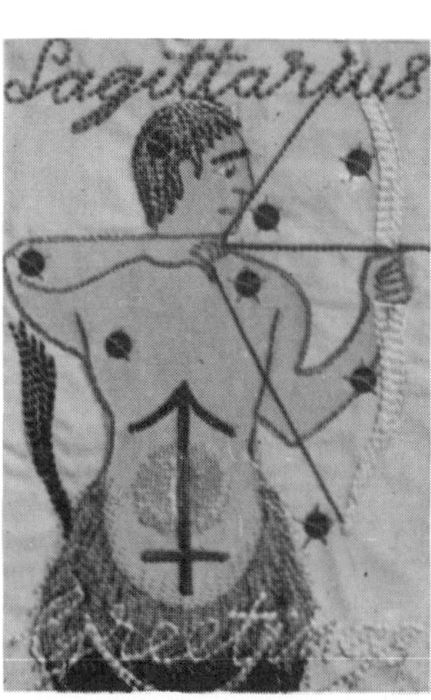

A Best Seller

In 1949 Lilian published a design for patchwork in the *Teachers World and Schoolmistress* in which the Planets and Zodiac Signs revolve around the sun, and three years later made a set of Zodiac birthday cards, each accompanied by its appropriate stone of the month, that proved so popular she became the Craft Centre's best selling embroiderer. She had already designed a number of Christmas cards and when they were written up by Alison Settle in *The Observer* and by Isabel Adam in *The Scotsman*, she was so overwhelmed with orders she had to enlist the help of the students in her machine embroidery class at Twickenham School of Art. She described her technique in the issue of *Needlework Illustrated* for November 1955:

Here is an idea that will appeal to all who appreciate the charm and quality of personally produced Christmas Cards. The general principal for machining is this: Wind Pearsall's Filoselle Silk onto an empty cotton reel (3 strands together, ie half the skein thickness), and use this on top of the machine, with machine twist on the shuttle; a large needle and a medium stitch will be needed. For contrast detail (the inner lines on holly leaves, for example) use twist both top and below, smaller needle and finer stitch. Machine all parts as continously as possible, lifting the foot when turns are needed – as is usual in machining. Before commencing the embroidery give body to the material by sticking it to thin cotton (old sheeting is excellent), using office or wallpaper paste. Press till dry.

Zodiac design from Teachers World **and** School Mistress

"Follow Me"

Study of St Peter

My Son's Saints

Ecclesiastical Affairs

Lilian made her first panel with a biblical subject in 1936. Still a newcomer to embroidery and its methods, she followed the instructions for applique work step by step. First, the drawing, then the tracing from it; the cutting out of the tracing into its component parts and the shaping of her materials around the pieces; the turning down of raw edges, and finally the stitching of everything together. But it proved too slow and irksome a way of working for her fast flowing ideas; she wanted greater freedom to change her mind as work proceeded than this allowed; and, asserting her independence, she added a little padding here and there. For the rest, she used speckled crash for the cliffs, pale blue silk with a watery pattern of wavy lines for the sea, and thick dark brown cloth, pleated to look like planking, for the boat.

Comparison of St Peter with the figures of St Matthew and St James in My Son's Saints of 1956, shows how completely her style changed in the intervening years. All she now uses are two identical rectangles, yellow gold on the left and turquoise blue on the right, and in front of them a shorter, broader rectangle in silver grey, and three circles, one a little smaller than the others. On top of this prepared background she draws the saints, using couched threads outlining them as she did years ago on the Thisbe and Peace... panels, and adding a scroll borrowed directly from the Angel and Demon on the blackout curtain and in Kindred Spirit, together with such essential accessories as St Matthew's money bags and custom house, and St James's fish and sailing boat. When exhibited at All Hallows, London Wall, it brought her a commission from Mowbray & Company, the ecclesiastical suppliers, for a cope, later acquired for St John the Evangelist, Montreal.

A combination of ruthless economy and flowing, calligraphic thread drawing has introduced a new element into ecclesiastical embroidery. These saints are strong, flesh and blood men, decisive, robust and determined, and derive neither from stained glass windows, illuminated manuscripts nor other embroidery of any period. Are they, I wonder, Druids impersonating saints, or actors taking part in one of the great medieval mystery plays in York, Chester or Norwich? Who knows? But there is no denying that the design on the hood with St Peter in direct confrontation with St Paul on either side of that centrally sited sword would make a splendid poster for a revival of any one of them, or that it is Lilian's early training in poster design that gives her church work its distinctive character.

After the Montreal cope there were commissions from local churches, including one for St Anne's , Kew Green,

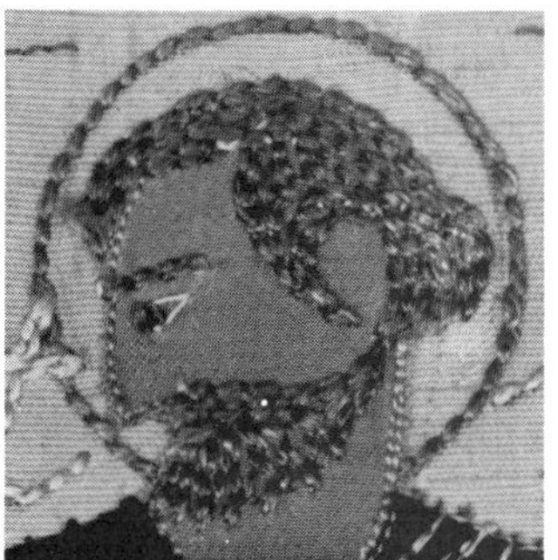

St Peter on Montreal Cope

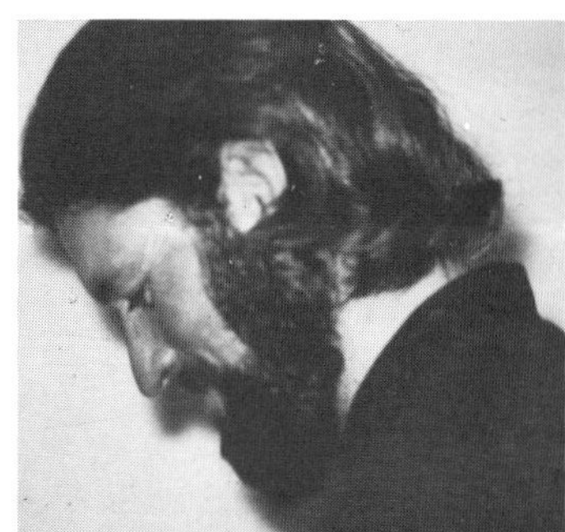

Matthew Dring c1972

Hood of Montreal Cope

of which a perceptive contributor to the *Richmond Herald* wrote: "Mrs Dring usually has an idea in mind when she sets out to work; the finished pattern or picture comes to her while working on the fabric."

In 1958 there was a major commission from Gloucester Cathedral for a set of green vestments, followed in 1962 by another for a white and gold set for festivals. It was for these that Lilian made the abstract designs referred to in the Foreword by Constance Howard. In the summer of 1988 the second set was included in an exhibition in the crypt of St Paul's Cathedral in celebration of the centenary of the Arts and Crafts Exhibition Society.

Fabric-House-Portraits

The idea for these came in the summer of 1956 when she stayed with friends in Wiltshire and Sussex and found their houses lent themselves perfectly to her style and method of working. Thereafter she usually made an architectural elevation from photographs as a preliminary and, after one unhappy experience, always insisted on a visit to the house, from which she returned with the shapes, textures, colours and surroundings fixed in her mind. Today it is hard to believe that she felt it was "cheating" to do a little dry brush painting on the red sandstone, lichen covered walls of a mansion in Dumfriesshire, that proved unmatchable in any fabric old or new.

Amongst the London Portraits she enjoyed was the Georgian terrace house in South Kensington that belonged to the Director of the Design Centre. She was dismayed however, to find he expected an exact replica of its wrought iron balcony and the old lamp post that effectively obscured part of it. Perhaps he was only trying her out on this. I understand he has it still and continues to enjoy it.

Rather less to her taste was a request for the penthouse running across the attics of two houses in Eaton Square, with features including 36 windows, some with pediments; 6 Doric columns between spearhead railings, that supported a balustraded balcony; and a cornice of rams'-heads at the top. She found the trees very useful.

Two houses near Henley-on-Thames gave her great pleasure. Grey's Green Farm came first, richly textured in flint and brick with a tiled roof, and the family home, Grey's Court, "a stupendous job," she says that took her over a hundred hours to complete. In 1969 when the estate was given to the National Trust, her Portrait became the Trust's official postcard, and an amended version of it appeared on the cover of the guide book.

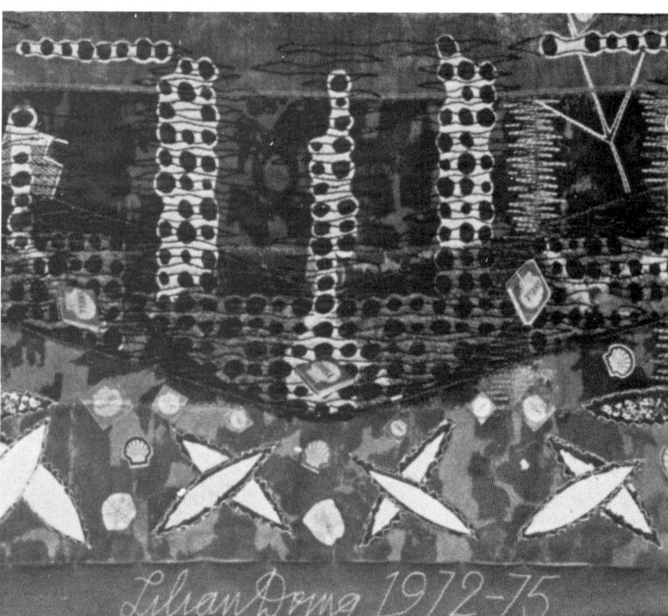

Parable 2

In 1972 Lilian embarked upon a second Parable. It measures 6 ft × 3 ft and took three years to complete.

Burdened in spirit by man's abuse of his evironment, she added a word to each of the three biblical quotations in Parable 1 and they became "the *polluted* heavens above", "the *over-populated* earth beneath" and "the *poisoned* waters under the earth".

At the top, immediately below the ring pulls from beer cans from which, with awful cynicism, she hung it, concordes have taken over what the poets once called the empyrean, and it is now defiled by rubbish cast out by satellites circling the world on their way to the planets. Airliners, thick as locusts, represented by blue cotton with a pattern of tiny diagonal lines, that criss cross and recross the sky, while in front, Harriers cut from advertisements in her local paper, trail black fumes behind them.

Below, a multi-windowed city, a man-made conglomorate with white ticker tape skyscrapers in the distance as far as the eye can see, and a patchwork of buildings in front put together from checked fabrics, the checks diminishing in size to give an illusion of scale and perspective.

The swathe of fast moving cars and lorries constructed from adhesive and other waste products with press-stud wheels, eastbound at the top, westbound below, all converging at high speed, regardless of their own or others' safety, upon a complexity of intersecting lanes, flyovers and spaghetti junctions. Hurriedly summoned motorway police and ambulances will soon be arriving at the horrendous pile up that inevitably happens. How much country has been lost to what we call Progress, she wonders? How many more woods will be defaced? How many forests cut down? Dead, bleached gladioli stems from her garden are her answer.

Soil erosion and the city's effluent turn the rivers brown; as the water supply runs out, banks appear as demands upon it increase. Oil leaking from tankers flows across the sea. When a tanker sinks oil gushes out in black bubbles. An upturned life boat indicates there are no survivors from the crew. Life on the seabed dies with them. Fish bones and the fur from her kettle are now her medium, punctuated by an oil company's logo.

So Parable 2 is a challenge, a warning and a banner the Ecology Movement might well make its own.

The End is the Beginning

In 1989 Lilian is to be accorded a retrospective exhibition at Orleans House Gallery, Twickenham. Only then will it be possible for us to realise the extent and variety of her work, and make a proper appraisal of the influence upon it of her early training in poster design. When this happens it is likely that the Music Cushions will be seen to be amongst the best things she has ever done. Persuaded to look at them with the cool detachment all embroiderers learn to bring their work before they decide it has reached an acceptable standard, Lilian admits they give her at least as much, if not rather more satisfaction than most.

But even now, with only the foregoing illustrations to guide us, we can draw some conclusions about her work.

The function of a poster is to convey a message and her Personal Pillows and Music Cushions are not the only pieces in which the design incorporates a hidden message, an attribution, that is for private rather than public interpretation.

Then, if the poster is to fulfil its function, the image must be completely simple, and it is characteristic of most of the embroideries in this book, that the designs are arrangements of simple geometric shapes, perfectly balanced, and brought into pleasing relationship with one another in order to fill a given shape.

John Farleigh, who rated her work so highly that he accepted whatever she offered him for sale in the Craft Centre, Hay Hill, – with the exception, of "Jessie Matthews" – declared that simplicity, which is so difficult to achieve, is the keynote of the best work of any period. "Without simplicity, without organised design," he wrote in 1956, the year in which Lilian made her second Music Cushion, "everything becomes confused, incoherent, unintelligible." Is this, we may wonder, the message of Parable 2?

In the same book, *Design for Applied Decoration in the Crafts*, he tells us something about those who purchased and commissioned Lilian's work through the Craft Centre. He describes them as discriminating people, who wished to decorate their homes with simple, well designed furnishings, with the sole object of making them pleasant to live in, and he welcomed this as evidence for "the continuation of our great tradition of Arts and Crafts, which is so closely associated with the art of living."

Lilian's commitment to the Arts and Crafts is total. It animates her whole being and inspires her designs. What I have designated as her Textile Graphics are truly "pleasant to live with", and what more than this could any embroiderer wish for?

Lilian is justifiably proud of having, by unremitting hard work, earned her living as a hand machine embroiderer, and of the collection of small hand-made books and folders in which she has kept a record of her work – the one of the House Portraits is particularly attractive, and the cover of another with a design based upon her script lettering is reproduced here as the outside back cover. Amongst the notes she gave me I found this account of its evolution and of her awareness of the continuity of the past:

Asked for a concluding message she wrote this: "I feel I have in some part conformed to my family forebears who were wrought-iron smiths in Mere, Wiltshire, for at least three generations, by *using* metal – pins, needles, scissors, sewing machine. By the same token, my machine script, evolved in 1947, an example of which is reproduced on the outside back cover, is a near-replica of my grandfather's signature in the Marriage Register of Mere Church, though I did not discover this until three or four years after I designed it."

Relevent events in arts, crafts and embroidery

1913	Omega Workshops opened by Roger Fry
1919	Bauhaus founded in Weimar. (Lilian's teachers at the Royal College of Art included Reco Capey, a product of the Bauhaus)
1920	British Institution for Industrial Art founded.
1921	Red Rose Guild of Art Workers founded in Manchester by Margaret Pilkington as authorative body maintaining standards and providing sales outlet.
1922	Retirement of Professor W R Lethaby, succeeded as Head of Design School at Royal College of Art by Professor E W Tristram.
1924	British Empire Exhibition at Wembley.
1925	L'Exposition des Arts Decoratifs, Paris.
1928	The Little Gallery founded in Sloane Square by Muriel Rose and Peggy Turnbull showing textiles by Ethel Mairet, Enid Marx, etc.
1932	Modern Embroidery Exhibition sponsored by British Institute for Industrial Art at Victoria and Albert Museum including work from continental countries.
1933	Bauhaus closes.
1934	Council for Art and Industry set up by Board of Trade, Chairman Frank Pick; Needlework Development Scheme set up in Glasgow by J and P Coats to encourage interest in embroidery and raise the standard of design.
1936	Dunbar Hay, Albemarle Street, founded by Cecilia Dunbar Kilburn and Athole Hay to put young designers from Royal College of Art in touch with manufacturers; firm specialised in well designed commercially produced goods but also stocked pottery, hand-blocked textiles and embroidery designs.
1938	Ethel Mairet becomes the first woman to receive the Royal Society of Arts "Royal Designer for Industry" award; 50th anniversary exhibition of the Arts and Crafts Exhibition Society at the Royal Academy; Scottish Women's Rural Institutes National Exhibition in Glasgow; Needlework Development Scheme closed until 1944.
1945	Henry Rothschild opens "Primavera" in Sloane Street.
1946	Arts Council founded. "British Can Make It Exhibition" organised by Council for Industrial Art included textiles by Marianne Straub.
1948	Arts Council Travelling Exhibition of work by Needlework Development Scheme.
1949	British Handcraft Export Centre set up by John. Farleigh, Forerunner of the Crafts Centre, Hay Hill. "Arts for All" exhibition of posters produced for London Transport 1908-49.
1950	Arts Council exhibition "Experiment in Embroidery Design" showing designs by Mary Kessell developed by students at Bromley School of Art.
1951	Festival of Britain.
1952	Arts Council exhibition "Pottery and Textiles 1920-52 "Made in Great Britain by Artist/Craftsmen. Dartington Hall".
1953	Arts Council exhibition "British Life" paintings showing life in Britain from Queen Elizabeth I to coronation of Queen Elizabeth II.
1955	"Craftsmanship Today" exhibition sponsored by Crafts Centre of Great Britain.
1955/56	Arts Council Travelling Exhibition of contemporary embroidery.
1956	Design Centre opened in The Haymarket.
1961	Needlework Development Scheme closes.
1963	Arts Council exhibition "Opus Anglicanum".
1964	First Habitat shop opened in London.
1976	"Tonic to the Nation" exhibition at Victoria and Albert Museum to celebrate 25th anniversary of the Festival of Britain.

Biographical Notes

1908	b Surbiton, Surrey
1916	Family moves to New Malden
1922 – 26	Kingston School of Art
1926 – 29	Royal College of Art
1930	Free lance graphic artist in Fleet Street: six months with press agency.
1931	Married James Dring, a painter/potter. Living at 32 South Side, Clapham Common, and began to experiment with applique embroidery for furnishings.
1932	First "Personal Pillow"
1934	Cushion cover in applique "Peasant Dance".
1935	First raised applique panel "Deep Sea Fishing". Shown at Dorland Hall. Invited to join Arts and Crafts Exhibition Society (now Society of Designer/Craftsmen).
1937	Showed "Personal Pillows", screen in applique, hand printed textiles, etc with Contemporary Georgians' exhibition at the Wertheim Gallery, Burlington Gardens.
1939 – 45	1942 birth of her son Matthew Dring now Head of Department of Marine Botany, Queen's University, Belfast. Part time C.D. warden. Wrote articles on needlework for *Teachers World and Schoolmistress*, and a series called "Thriftcraft" for *Arts and Craft Education*. Ideas for economy crafts, toys, games etc for teachers. Taught at Occupational Therapy Centre, Swiss Cottage. Commissions for John Lewis Partnership.
1942	Work exhibited by British council in USA and Canada.
1946	Re-designed "Rouget" packaging for Coty. Devised road safety game for RoSPA. Wrote and Illustrated 4 *Nursery-Versery Books*, published by Collins.
1947	Started to do hand machine stitched applique using 1912 Frister/Rossman machine. Founder member of the Craft Centre of Great Britain.
1950	Awarded prize in European Recovery Programme Poster Competition (British Section).
1951	Organised "Women of the Century" exhibition and directed making of "Patchwork of the Century", shown at Festival of Britain, South Bank exhibition.
1951 – 61	Part-time teaching at Richmond Institute of Further Education and Twickenham School of Art.
1952	Works shown in Arts Council exhibition "Pottery and Textiles 1920 – 52 Made in Great Britain by Artist/Craftsmen" at Dartington Hall, Devon, and Arts and Crafts Exhibition Society's selection, Florence. First embroidered Birthday and Christmas Cards.
1955	Work exhibited with Crafts Centre selection in New Zealand.
1956	First Fabric-House-Portrait
1957	First commission for ecclesiastical embroidery.
1958	Commission for a set of Trinity vestments for Gloucester Cathedral.
1961	Exhibition at Richmond Library.
1962	Commission for set of festal vestments for Gloucester Cathedral. Trinity set exhibited at Coventry Festival.
1965	Part-time teaching at Geffrye Museum.
1966	Part-time teaching in craft workshops at Star and Garter Home, Richmond.
1967	Retrospective exhibition at All Hallows, London Wall.
1977	"Arts in the Church"; loan exhibition, Kingston Parish Church. Organisers: Nancy Tatham (convenor), Lilian Dring (designer) and Rosemary Pedder.
1987	Retrospective exhibition at Museum and Heritage Centre, Kingston.
1988	Participation in London Exhibitions for Centenary of Arts and Crafts Exhibition Society.